W9-ALM-570

Mosquito

Jill Bailey

Heinemann Library
Des Plaines, Illinois

j595.772
BAI

© 1998 Reed Educational & Professional Publishing
Published by Heinemann Library,
an imprint of Reed Educational & Professional Publishing,
1350 East Touhy Avenue, Suite 240 West
Des Plaines, IL 60018

Customer Service 1-888-454-2279

All rights reserved. No part of this publication may be reproduced or transmitted in any form
or by any means, electronic or mechanical, including photocopying, recording, taping, or any
information storage and retrieval system, without permission in writing from the publisher.

Designed by Celia Floyd
Illustrations by Alan Male
Printed in Hong Kong

02 01 00 99
10 9 8 7 6 5 4 3 2

Library of Congress Cataloging-in-Publication Data

Bailey, Jill.
    Mosquito / Jill Bailey
        p.   cm. -- (Bug books)
        Includes bibliographical references and index.
        Summary: A simple introduction to the physical characteristics,
    diet, life cycle, predators, habitat, and lifespan of mosquitoes.
        ISBN 1-57572-663-7 (lib. bdg.)
        1. Mosquitoes--Juvenile literature. [1. Mosquitoes.] I. Title.
    II. Series
    QL536.B2 1998
    595.77'2--dc21   98-10596
                                                          CIP
                                                          AC

Paperback ISBN 1-57572-459-6

Acknowledgments
The Publishers would like to thank the following for permission to reproduce photographs:
Ardea London: R. Gibbons p. 7, D. Greenslade p. 4; Bruce Coleman: J. Shaw p. 6, K. Taylor p. 13; FLPA:
D. Grewcock p. 11, L West p. 21; Chris Honeywell p. 28; NHPA: G. Bernard pp. 15, 17, 20, S. Dalton
pp. 26, 27, P. Parks p. 9, J. Shaw p. 23; Oxford Scientific Films: R. Brown p. 22, J. Cooke pp. 10, 14, 16, 18,
19; London Scientific Films: p. 12, H. Taylor p. 29; Planet Earth Pictures: A. Mounter p. 24; Science Photo
Library: T. Brain p. 5, A. Crump p. 25, J. Revy. Cover photograph reproduced with permission of child:
Chris Honeywell; mosquito: Geof du Feu, Planet Earth Pictures.

Every effort has been made to contact copyright holders of any material reproduced in this book. Any
omissions will be rectified in subsequent printings if notice is given to the Publisher.

Any words appearing in the text in bold, **like this**, are explained in the Glossary.

Contents

What are mosquitoes?

Mosquitoes are **insects**. They have a body made up of three parts—a head, a middle, and an **abdomen**. They have three pairs of legs and one pair of wings.

A mosquito has big eyes. It also has
a pair of **antennae** for touching,
smelling, and hearing. Baby mosquitoes
are little wriggling grubs. They live in
water.

Where do mosquitoes live?

Mosquitoes live in damp shady places near pools of water where their babies can live. Even small puddles are big enough for mosquito babies to live in.

Mosquitoes often come into houses and rest on walls or ceilings. They live all over the world, especially in **tropical** forests and in the far north.

What do mosquitoes look like?

Mosquitoes are small **insects**. The common house mosquito is only about as long as a little fingernail. The males are thinner than the females and have feathery **antennae**.

Mosquitoes fly in a jerky up-and-down way, with their legs hanging below them. They rest with their wings folded. There are more than 1,600 different kinds of mosquitoes in the world.

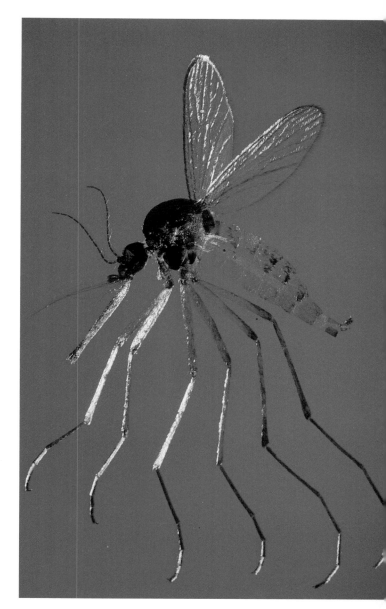

What do mosquitoes do?

Many mosquitoes hide during the day. They come out in the evening when the air is cool and damp. They look for food and other mosquitoes.

Crowds of male mosquitoes "dance"
together to attract the females. The
males' **antennae** listen for the whine
of the females' wings. The male and
female mosquitoes **mate**.

How long do mosquitoes live?

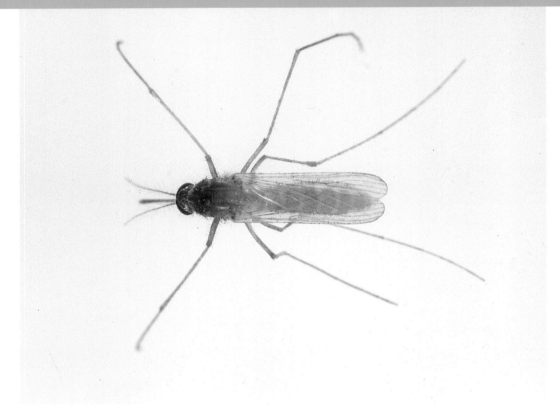

The female mosquitoes live longest, sometimes for two to three weeks. A few mosquitoes live much longer. They **hibernate** through the cold winter in houses or **hollow** trees.

These mosquitoes lay their eggs in water in the spring and then die. In less than a month there will be new adult mosquitoes ready to lay their own eggs.

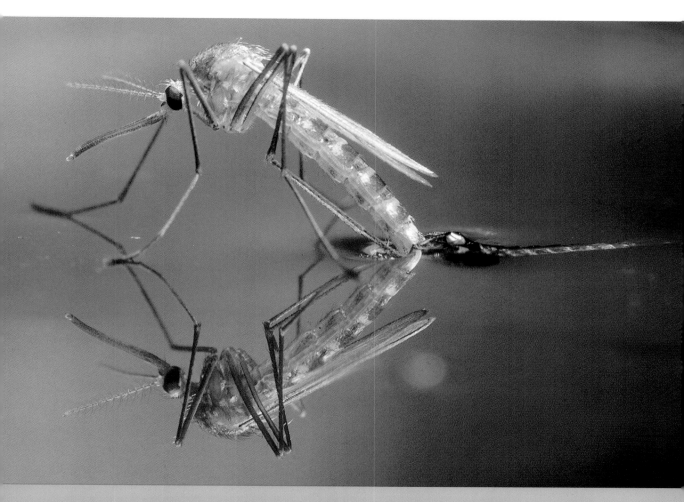

How are mosquitoes born?

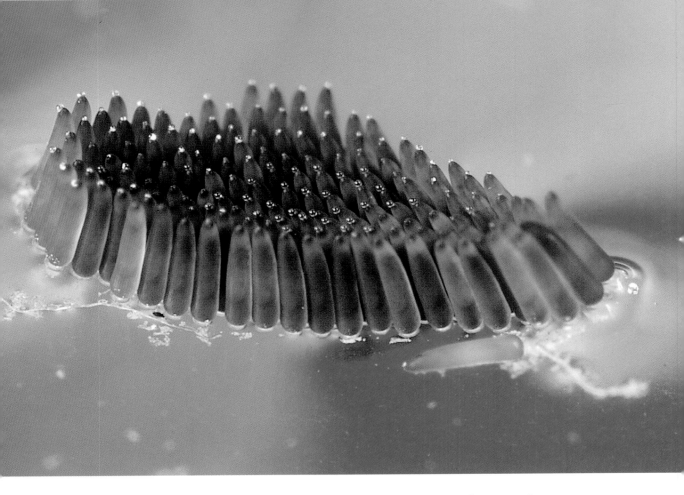

The female house mosquito lays her eggs on the surface of a small pond or puddle. She lays up to 300 eggs at a time. They form a tiny **raft**.

After a few hours, the eggs **hatch**. A
tiny wriggling **larva** escapes through
the bottom of each egg and swims away.

How do mosquitoes grow?

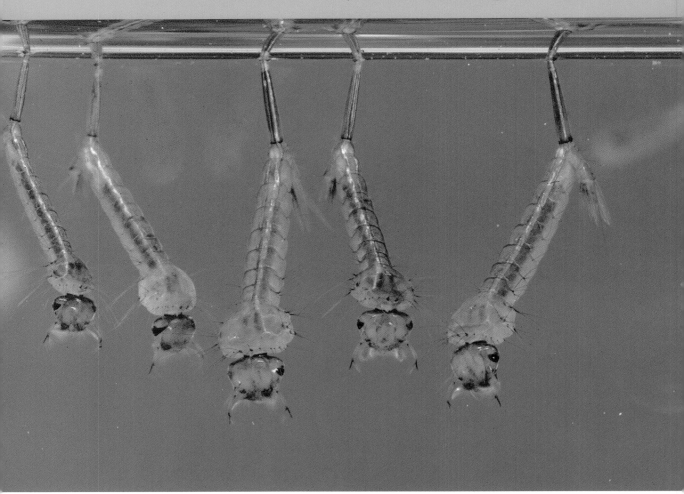

Baby mosquito **larvae** hang upside-down from the water surface. They breathe in air through a long tube. They can swim by wriggling.

The little larva's mouth is surrounded by hairs. These hairs sweep water into the mouth. The larva eats tiny pieces of food floating in the water.

17

How do baby mosquitoes change shape?

When a **larva** gets big enough it stops eating. Its head end gets very large and grows two little trumpets to take in air. It is now called a **pupa**.

Inside its skin, the pupa slowly changes into an adult mosquito. The skin splits and the new mosquito climbs out and flies away.

What do mosquitoes eat?

Adult mosquitoes do not eat much. They suck up flower **nectar** through their long mouths. Female mosquitoes drink blood to help them make eggs.

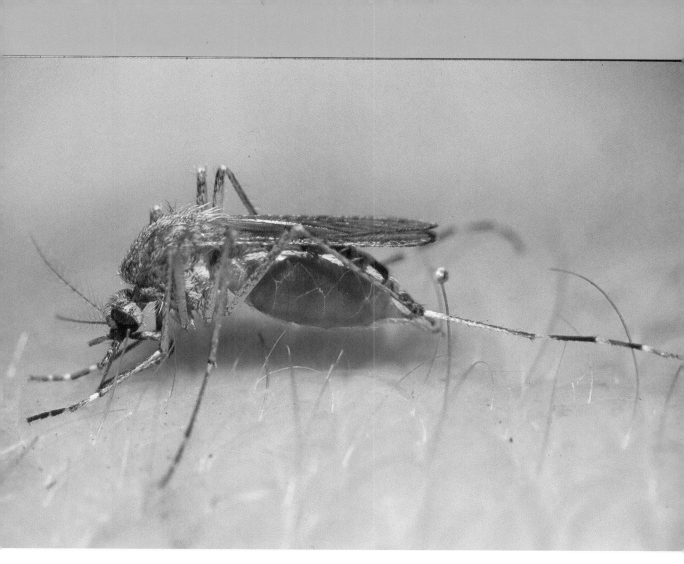

The female mosquito breaks the skin of an animal or person with her sharp mouth. Then she adds a juice to stop the blood from **clotting** as she feeds. This juice may make the bite itch.

Which animals attack mosquitoes?

Many birds eat mosquitoes. They also feed them to their young. Millions of birds fly to the far north in summer because so many mosquitoes live there.

Frogs, toads, rats, and mice also eat mosquitoes. Spiders catch them in their webs. Fish, water beetles, and dragonfly **larvae** eat baby mosquitoes.

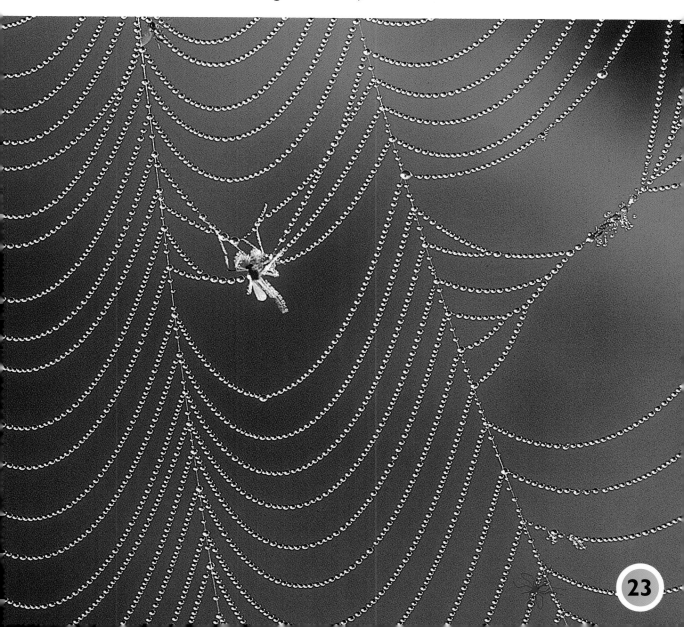

How are mosquitoes special?

Mosquitoes are important food for birds and other animals. They can also cause harm. In some countries, mosquitoes spread disease, so people spray **chemicals** to kill them.

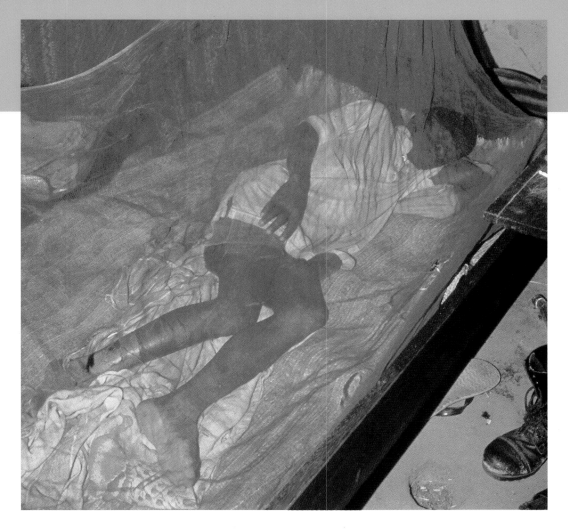

When a female mosquito sucks blood, she may carry diseases from one person or animal to another. In some countries, people sleep under special nets so they will not be bitten.

How do mosquitoes move?

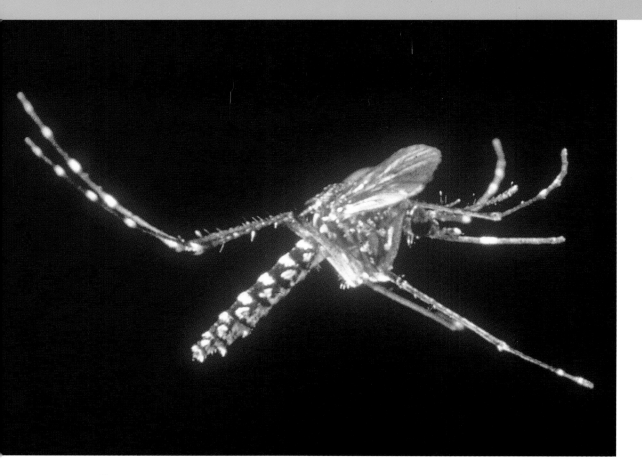

Grown-up mosquitoes fly. A mosquito can fly very long distances in search of food. It can flap its wings up to 600 times a second.

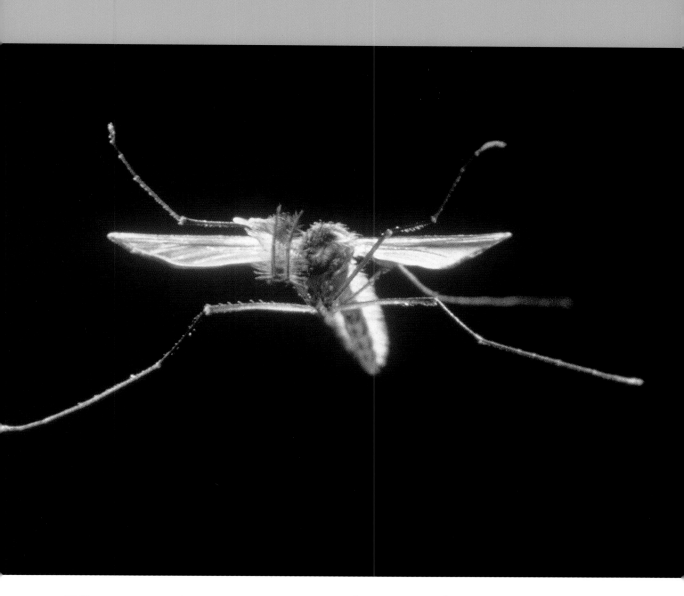

The moving wings make a whining noise. Males and females move their wings at different speeds. They make different whining noises.

Thinking about Mosquitoes

Are there any large puddles or buckets of water near your home? Are there any tiny **rafts** of mosquito eggs in them?

Do you think there are more mosquitoes after it rains or after it has been dry for awhile? Why?

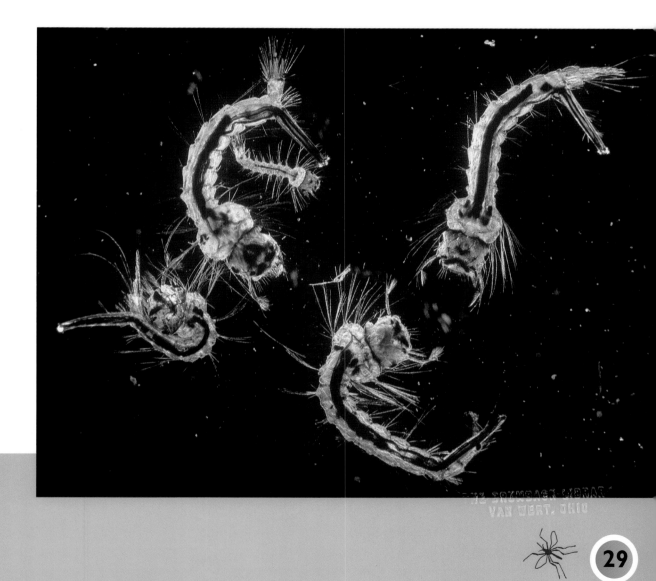

THE BRUMBACK LIBRARY
VAN WERT, OHIO

Mosquito Map

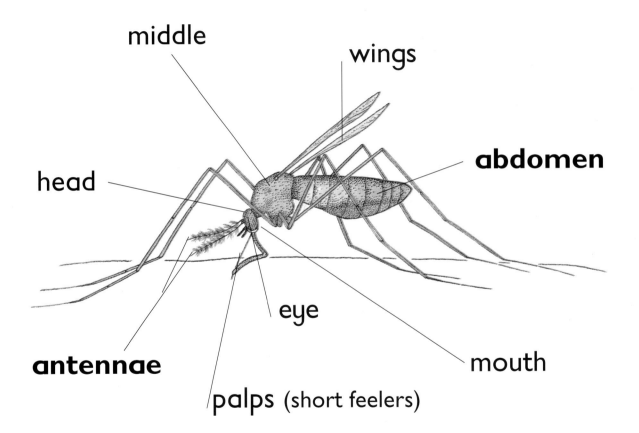

middle

wings

abdomen

head

antennae

eye

palps (short feelers)

mouth

Glossary

abdomen the tail-end of an insect

antenna (More than one are called **antennae**) long bendy rods that stick out from the head of an insect. They may be used to feel, smell, or hear. Sometimes they are covered in tiny hairs.

to come out of the egg

chemicals when blood becomes thick, then hard, to form a scab that stops more bleeding

hatch to be born out of an egg

hibernate a very long sleep some animals have that lasts all winter

hollow a hollow tree is usually dead and the trunk is empty inside

insect a small animal with six legs

larva (more than one are called **larvae**) the grub that hatches from the egg

mate a male and female mosquito come together to make baby mosquitoes

nectar a sweet juice inside flowers

pupa (more than one are called **pupae**) step between larva and adult

raft something that is flat and can float on the surface of water

tropical parts of the world that are hot and wet

31

More Books to Read

Patent, Dorothy H. *Mosquitoes*. New York: Holiday House, 1986. An older reader can help you read this book.

Index